FULLNESS OF

Joy

WHEN THE WOUNDS OF YOUR HEART

ARE FILLED WITH Gold

Stephanie Rene' Claiborne

Forward with Liz Wright

FIRST EDITION
Heart of Gold Publishing
3705 Arctic Boulevard
#2233
Anchorage, Alaska 99503-5774

ISBN: -10-0-692-94750-0
ISBN-13:978-0-692-94750-0

Cover art and graphic design by David Stoddard: Website: http://mediarevelation.com/ Email: dave@graphicassault.com
Interior format design by Marie Fowler: mariefowlerlivingstones@gmail.com.

Author website: www.heartofgoldministries.com
Email: stephanie@heartofgoldministries.com

DEDICATION

To my mother.
Thank you for loving me and for teaching me to
never take anything for granted. My life
wouldn't be the same without you.

CONTENTS

FORWARD
with Liz Wright

To become utterly transformed into the exact likeness of Jesus is the purpose of the true Christian life. The Apostle Paul lays this incredible truth before us in Ephesians 4:24; '*You were created to be like God in all righteousness and holiness.*' All of Heaven is invested in this purpose. Jesus will have the desire of His heart, the reward of His sufferings; a people made in His own image, clothed in His nature, radiating His light, a people full of love and power.

As we become convinced of this amazing truth it changes how we view all that we are and every person we meet. It enables us to rightly align to the challenges and heart break. It begins to disempower the hopelessness that engulfs us as we struggle to make sense of our pain and suffering.

With this understanding we begin to see that through the redeeming power of the Cross the struggles and pain in life are forced to become our escort into the deeper life of true union with the heart of our Creator. Everything becomes purposeful in this Divine objective. Nothing in our lives remains outside of Jesus' redemptive plan.

As we begin to increasingly live in this place of true divine exchange we taste the truth that Paul also famously teaches us in II Corinthians 12: 9-10. That every single difficulty and weakness in life is now a doorway into experiencing God's transformational power. It's where we find the gold!

This is the heart of this incredible book and the gift we receive as we begin to immerse ourselves in the life-changing wisdom within its pages. In it Stephanie vulnerably and openly shares from her life, imparting to us the treasures she has learned that once applied will have a transformational impact in your own.

Stephanie is a woman of great love and humility who has reached out through tremendous pain and discovered God to be all He claims to be! Her testimony provides us with hope and keys to begin to engage the more that is available to each of us, no matter what we are facing. You will feel not only Stephanie's love but also through her anointed words the Fathers also, inviting you to trust and let go and allow Him to show you the Truth, that can truly heal you and set you free.

-Liz Wright
Author Ekklesia Rising
Founder & Senior Director of The Bridal Company

ACKNOWLEDGMENTS

My Ashley girl. I am so amazed by you and how you have blessed my life. From the time that Heaven gave you to me, to all of the times that you and I laugh and talk on the phone, there has been pure joy. I cannot thank you enough for your laughter, your love and your ability to see the bigger picture. I can't thank God enough for the ability to raise you and for you to call me your mother.

Michael and Juanita Claiborne. Thank you for always encouraging me and believing in me. You both have enriched my life in more ways than I can count.

My beloved friends,

Jane Malnoske, you are one of my dearest and loveliest friends. You have been with me through thick and thin and somehow, we always have found a way to laugh. God has used you to impart deep spiritual knowledge and insight into my life and I wouldn't be where I am today without this. Every adventure, every conversation, every declaration and prayer has impacted my life deeply. I love you and I am so happy to call you my friend.

Barbara Kay, my journey with the Father began with your guidance and love. Your genuineness and love is unparalleled. Thank you for pushing those around you into the Father's embrace.

Susan Wright, you are an amazing light in my life. You are someone that has taught me the value in going after the gold and how I am able to press in to the glory that God has for us. Thank you for your patience, your love, and your persistence in chasing after God. You are truly loved!

Marie Fowler, thank you for praying for me and with me on a weekly basis in order to bring this writing project to life. Our prayer times have meant the world to me and I am so pleased to call you my friend.

Michael and Margaret Malnoske, I can't even begin to tell you how much the both of you mean to me. When there was no one to call mother and father, you two were there and stepped in as my mother and father. Your kindness, care, and deep love in my life have been a mainstay and an example of how a mother and father should be.

Jonas Lohner, Meredith Lemely, and Jordan Parish. You three were instrumental in bringing this book to the surface. Thank you for laughing with me, crying with me, and dreaming with me.

Jennifer Miskov, thank you for teaching me to dream and to bring my dreams to others. Your anointing and destiny has brought hope to so many of us. I am truly blessed by you and I can't thank you enough for your encouragement and belief in me.

Sherri Dodd and Paula Malvo-Allen, your steadfast love for me has shaped how I see others and how I believe ministry should flow. You both are an amazing teachers, mothers, and mentors. Thank you for always being open to the supernatural and what the Father is doing.

Liz Wright, I cannot find the words to thank you for everything that I have been able to obtain from your ministry to the bride.

Bethel School of Supernatural Ministry, thank you for each and every one of your instructors and for opening the door to the impossible. I will forever be grateful.

ENDORSEMENTS

Fullness of Joy is sure to release fresh hope to every wounded soul. We've all experienced hard times in our lives and Stephanie does an incredible job of demonstrating the compassion and redemption of God. As she shares some of her own God stories so vulnerably, you are sure to be encouraged and realize like never before that God is always with you and working on your behalf. Stephanie is a woman of great love. I pray that as you receive this gift from her heart that your soul is healed, restored, strengthened, and awakened to even more of the beauty in Jesus that awaits.

-Jennifer A. Miskov, PhD, author and founding director of Destiny House

I want to recommend this wonderful book on inner healing. It is a tremendous testimony of real and lasting fruit from the recent outpouring of revival in Redding, CA and its effect on one particular life. Mrs. Claiborne unashamedly bares her soul, describing in painful yet inspiring detail how the Lord can transform the heart, renew the mind, redeem one's past and solidify each believer in their identity in Christ. If you are looking for practical help in the area of inner healing and pursuing your destiny in Christ, this book is tailor made for you.

-Michael Major
Author, *The Glory - Its Nature and End-Time Purpose* and Worship Leader of *Glory Encounter*

Fullness of Joy is a great read. Stephanie unlocks the truth that we can encounter the Father so profoundly that wholeness and healing will be released to the wounded or broken places in our hearts. This book is well written, engaging, has strong scriptural support, and has many practical examples to help the reader relate the truths to their own lives. I highly recommend it.

-Steve Backlund
Igniting Hope Ministries

Daniel Chalmers and I have had the joy and honor of knowing Stephanie for the past two years. Our lives are so much richer thru this friendship. She sacrificially sowed and served Love Wins Ministries when she was attending Bethel school of supernatural ministry. She is an emerging voice in our generation. With a profound and powerful personal testimony of overcoming trauma, coupled with professional training, as well as her rich deep history in the Lord, her very life testifies that when God restores something — it's greater than the original. Nothing is impossible for the one who exchanges beauty for ashes and sets us all as His trophies of grace. This book carries keys that took decades for her to earn. May you go on a journey of encountering the heart of the father as you read the pages that lie before you...she has labored a lifetime for the chapters that await you! As you read, may you put a full demand on heaven to receive everything Jesus died for!!!

-Shara and Daniel Chalmers
Love Wins Ministries

Fullness Of Joy is a heartfelt writing born out of the Word of God and the very heart of the writer, Stephanie Claiborne. She writes with passionate truth through her own personal journey of experiences. This author makes it very plain of the healing power found in God and the willingness of the participator. This captive reading teaches (us) how we will benefit more from God by allowing Him to walk with us through each circumstance as He delicately fills our wounds with love and a purifying gold in our hearts. Stephanie has captured one of the most amazing attributes of God Himself and that is the mystery of His very Divine Redemptive graces towards us who believe.

-Jimmie Reed, Ph.D.
Senior Leader of Global Manifestations
Denver, Colorado

INTRODUCTION

I came upon the title of this book simply through an encounter with the Lord while I was a first-year student in ministry school. I knew the Lord was revealing my true identity, but I knew very little about inner healing. There is so much I am still learning about inner healing. I know now that wonderful process begins in the deep recesses of our hearts as we are truly wrapped in His kindness. I know now that His grace has been there through all of what I have gone through. I remember being a young girl and not having what I needed for my emotional needs to be met. This left an open wound in my heart and soul which later turned into behaviors that were out of control and sometimes dangerous. **BUT GOD**...This is absolutely where I could see the kind hand of the Father nurturing and caring for me even while I was still in another place other than wholeness. This leads me to when I was able to encounter the Father in a manner that brought true wholeness and healing into my life as well.

Having the Father's gold fill each wound of my heart has been essential to my growth and ministry. I am able to see how the Father wants all of humanity to come into healing and wholeness. When our hearts are healed, there is no doubt that we know who we are in heaven's eyes. We now are truly set free to impart our victory to others. I look at the life of Jesus and His ministry here on earth and I can see how He went about exchanging the wounds that people had in their souls and in their hearts with pure gold. We see this exchange in the woman with the issue of blood, the demoniac, the people that were healed, and those that interacted with Jesus such as His disciples. Each of them had their own special interaction with Him. And all were able to walk in wholeness after they encountered their

Savior.

It is also my intention that whoever reads this book may encounter the Father in manner that brings him or her closer to the Father's heart. I remember always being drawn to old pictures of Jesus and Him pointing to His heart. I remember being a young child and thinking to myself, "I want to be in the center of His heart" and not really understanding what I was thinking or saying. I just knew that I wanted to be in His heart and I wanted to be close to Him. God wants us to be in His heart, and He wants to encounter us in a manner that breaks off the lies that we have accumulated about ourselves and others. He stated in the beginning that we were made in His image, the image of wholeness, love, kindness, longsuffering, joy, and peace. We were meant to walk in a way that glorifies His name and who He is as our heavenly Father.

All of this is to say GET READY to become whole! GET READY to become joyful! GET READY to step into understanding and Peace as He has determined to fill every place in your heart with GOLD!

CHAPTER 1

WHEN THE WOUNDS OF YOUR HEART ARE FILLED WITH *Gold*

*"I am also learning that as those places becoming mended (or **filled with gold**, so to speak), we are then pushed up to a higher level of consciousness as to who we are and who God created us to be."*

CHAPTER 1
WHEN THE WOUNDS OF YOUR HEART
ARE FILLED WITH *Gold*

Lately, I have been on a journey as I discover more of who I am and what my destiny is to be. I definitely can say that as I move forward in this journey, I am learning more about the human heart (emotions) and how the body, mind and spirit will work in conjunction with our Creator to mend those broken places. I am also learning that as those places becoming mended (or filled with gold, so to speak), we are then pushed up to a higher level of consciousness as to who we are and who God created us to be. Let me explain.

One day, not too long ago, I was praying and making certain declarations over my life. I was asking God to heal my heart, to give me a heart of gold. This was truly a deep desire of mine as I was asking God to make up the deficits in my emotions and in my heart. I was watching how God was doing wonderful things in me and how it seemed as though I was really "in sync" for the first time ever. I was losing weight, giving and being a more solid part of my community and moving in what I felt was God's way of bringing me more in line with His will for my life. This process would actually help my heart to heal in more ways than one. God would actually allow me to engage His presence and enter into an encounter that I will not soon forget (I'll explain later).

When we think of the wounds of the heart, we think about those things that may hurt us to the core. For me, this wounding happened a long time ago as a child. You see, I grew up in a single parent household with my mother. My mother's intentions were always to do her best, but there were just issues that stood in her way such as mental illness. Due to this and other reasons, I grew up feeling like a part of me wasn't loved, like part of me wasn't good enough for my father to be around. Growing up, my self-esteem was low and I was generally a shy child. I didn't really stand up for myself and I sometimes would be bullied in school. I remember wishing that I had a father who would come and pick me up from school. I wished that, as he picked me up from school, he would end up defending me and telling those kids to leave me alone. That of course never happened.

As I became older, this lack of a father figure left me looking to be loved by the wrong people. The statistics you hear about people who grow up without a parental figure are really true. Their lives are often out of control and sometimes young girls, without fathers, will demonstrate risky and unsafe behaviors. This was certainly true in my case, and led me to a life that was out of control and I was emotionally up and down.

What I realized was that I needed to reach out to my biological father. I had to find him, as I thought this would change my life. I would no longer feel like an orphan (as an adult, my mother had passed away). I was able to pull some things together in my life after the passing of my mother, but I still longed for that place in my heart to be filled...and it wasn't.

An encounter that I had in early July 2015 brought some perspective to my situation. I had a dream where I was brought into what I thought was God's heart. His heart was big and expansive. I felt such love and peace as I walked inside of His heart. I had noticed that along the walls of His heart were lines and cracks that were filled with what looked like gold. I ran my hands along the walls of his heart and said, "I never knew that your heart was wounded." He replied, "It isn't. This is your heart. I filled those wounded and cracked places with gold." When I woke up, I felt as though I was actually healing from deep heartache.

On July 6, 2015 (29 years to the day), I found a letter in an old box that was packed away. This letter was from my biological father that had information about a brother and an aunt. It was a miracle that I had found this letter, as this letter was mailed to me the year that I graduated from High School in 1986 and was a letter congratulating me on becoming an adult. The letter contained contact information, such as a mailing address for an aunt who lived in Detroit. Needless to say, I looked up this aunt's information and was able to talk to her over the phone. Amazingly, this aunt hadn't moved and was very happy to speak to me when I called her. We both cried together when I told her I was her niece.

In short, my father called me a few days later, and we were able to reunite with each other. I couldn't believe how all of those days, months, and years that were filled with such heartache had vanished. I finally felt that my father wanted me, and I felt very warm in my heart for him.

On October 23, 2015, I flew to Michigan to see family and to meet my brother and my sister whom I had never met. I also was able to spend much needed time with my father. I finally, as an adult, was able to communicate with him face to face for the first time. This was truly a healing event in my life where the wound of my heart was filled with gold.

I only tell you this information to encourage you. Either you or someone you may know has deep wounds of the heart that have yet to be healed. In my current occupation in the counseling profession, I have been able to see how when the wounds that we acquire as young children, teenagers, or as adults are not cared for and healed, we then will walk through our lives looking to fill those places that cause us pain with things that will numb the pain.

It is interesting to me as an adult (who is still walking through a healing journey), that many areas are overlooked and passed off as "normal" or just part of life. I am convinced that we are to live lives that are full of life and light. The only way to do this is to begin to nurture those parts of ourselves that are lacking in proper care and alignment. Just think of the places we can allow God to fill with gold! There are a lot of places like this. Sometimes those places are not necessarily big gaping wounds. Even seemingly small and insignificant wounds can profoundly alter how we think of ourselves and how we see others.

   I remember when I first became a case worker for those that were involved in social services. I had a hard time understanding how to assist people in their healing journey. It seemed as though they didn't want to be bothered in addressing the deep areas of their heart/personality. When I was speaking to my supervisor about this issue, she stated that something to me that is found in nature itself. She stated that when an animal, becomes wounded, it will hide. It will go into a cave. It will hide to protect itself. This was like it was a deep understanding that I hadn't thought about as it pertains to humans. We often will do the same thing. We will hide from friends, family, ourselves, and from God. This is where God wants to heal us so that we are seen and known not seen and known for our wounds but for who we are supposed to be.

CHAPTER 2

GIVE PEOPLE THE *Gold*

AND NOT THE DIRT

"…as I give God the pain, the hurt, and everything else. I am actually giving Him my whole heart,"

GOLD has been on my mind lately. I've come to realize (maybe I've always known this), that there is a lot of dirt in the process of digging for gold. When we dig for gold, we have to move the dirt from one place to another. The dirt has to be agitated and shaken. Then, usually, you will find flakes of gold with the occasional gold nugget mixed in with the dirt, mud and water.

When it comes to finding the gold in my own life, I have had to go through a similar process. One of the things that I've experienced in the digging process is that it hurts a little, and sometimes a lot. I've talked to others who have also said that this process has been a painful one, as they've allowed the dirt that is covering the gold to be exposed. This process is really messy and it is truly hard work as the dirt is being removed, the gold sifted and the process agitated.

Speaking of my own experiences, I have had times while searching for the gold in my own life where I had to move the dirt around and out of the way (gossip, hurt, disappointment, self-hatred, etc.). I have also noticed that sometimes the dirt wasn't put there by us or our life experiences, but we are still responsible for recognizing the dirt and getting it OUT of the way.

There is a process that will usually come after the gold has been found. It's called the refining process. I'll explain more later.

When I first dedicated my life to my Creator, I was a wreck. I had decided to stop using substances that hid my authentic self, and I was also in the process of grieving my mother's death. She had died of Alzheimer's disease. During this process, I cried a lot and was constantly in the scriptures, where I found solace. As I was looking for the gold in the refining process (which is an ongoing process) I would notice that everything that was previously suppressed in my life was coming to the surface. There were times when the hurt and pain

CHAPTER 2

GIVE PEOPLE THE *Gold* AND NOT THE DIRT

was so raw that this is what people encountered from me. Thank God for those in my life that loved me through it all.

God moved me into understanding the process and it felt as though a door of understanding had opened up for me. I learned how to give THE GOLD and not the dirt, so to speak. I am still learning that my actions, which are often generated by past hurts and disappointments, do not need to be passed on to others.

God is the one to Whom I choose to lay down the dirt of my life. This is why the actions of the cross are not in vain for me.

There is scripture which speaks to me about this process. It is found in Proverbs 3:5-8. It states:

> *Trust in the Lord with all of your heart and do not lean on your understanding, in all your ways acknowledge Him, and He will make your paths straight. Do not be wise in your own eyes; Fear the Lord and turn away from evil. It will be healing to your body and refreshment to your bones.*

This scripture absolutely rings true to me, and indeed I have found healing for my heart. This process will continue for the rest of my life as I give God the pain, the hurt, and everything else. I am actually giving Him my whole heart, meaning the happy heart, the sad heart, and everything in between. In this refining process, the goldsmith will heat up the gold until it melts into a liquid form. When gold is heated to the right temperature, the impurities come to the surface and are then skimmed off the top. This process continues until the impurities are gone. The goldsmith can then see his reflection in the gold. This is why the "process"

24

is so important. I want God to be able to see His
reflection in me. This truly produces a heart of gold.

CHAPTER 3

I LOOK LIKE MY *Father* ...

NO REALLY, I DO

*"Our lives are to reflect **who** we are and **whose** we are."*

WHO AM I?

I have always had issues with my identity and how I saw myself, even though my family's ethnic background was talked about frequently. I remember my mother telling me when I was much younger; "We are Cherokee Indian, Spanish, Scottish, Ethiopian and something else from another African country." Even though these different ethnic blends were in my blood, I never really felt a belonging to anywhere yet felt connected to everywhere. It was interesting to me that I would find myself drawn to various ethnic groups, and sometimes people would ask me if I was from the Dominican Republic, Samoa (or the Pacific Islands), or various other places. Even though this would happen on a regular basis, there still was no feeling of personal belonging.

EARLY YEARS

When I was in elementary school, the same kids who teased me would also wonder about my ethnic identity. Some of the kids would call me a Zebra or Oreo (Oreo meant that I was black on the outside but white on the inside). Really? Where does this come from? It makes me think now that our identity is attacked at a young age to make us unsure of who we are and the calling on our lives (I'll explain more later).

During these years of early childhood I would often long to have a father, my father, in my life. I was very young but still very aware of my situation. Ideally, I should have had a father, there to instill into me who I am.

Not having one certainly caused my heart to be wounded. Little did I know that in spite of all this, the Lord would heal my heart 40 years later. I think that having the right people in your life can become like a healing balm to your heart, to your identity, whereas the wrong people can be as poison to the soul.

I LOOK LIKE MY *Father*... NO I REALLY DO

Many of us may embrace various identities because of other people's ideas and preconceived notions about us. Sometimes, we could decide that it's easier to take on the identity that is spoken over us and to us, because we are unsure of who we really are. Now mind you, not everyone has this issue. I have met people who have similar circumstances who did not experience what I did. However, there are those who can identify personally, or know someone who is in a similar circumstance. For me, this lack of identity and feeling of unworthiness manifested in behaviors that were self-destructive. These self-destructive behaviors such as drug and alcohol abuse and, risky behaviors in relationships. almost succeeded in destroying me. Not knowing my worth or value, I would sometimes wish that I would die.

STEPPING INTO A NEW REALITY

Shortly after coming to Redding, California to attend school at Bethel School of Supernatural Ministry, I had a dream encounter with My Heavenly Father. In my dream, I was in the Garden with Him and he had spoken to my spirit about going to the well to draw fresh water. I looked inside the well and saw my reflection, as well as the reflections of the Heavenly Father, and a lamb. In my dream I was overcome with deep feelings of love and began to weep with gratification. Then, the Father spoke to my spirit and said, "See, you look just like Me." At that moment I awoke to a new reality; the realization that I am a child of the Most High God. He is my Father and I am complete. Shortly after this dream I was able to make contact with my earthly father. I made immediate arrangements to meet him in person. At that same meeting I met my sister, brother and multiple cousins.

I looked at my family members that I met for

the first time and could see a very strong family resemblance. But when I sat with my father, my sister took a picture of the both of us, the resemblance was uncanny. I looked just like my father. Later that same day, I met my brother for the first time. I knew and realized that what was spoken to my spirit that night was true. My brother told me that I really do look like all of the family members. I cried in my brother's arms as I finally felt a sense of belonging, and realized my Creator's faithfulness.

WALKING IN MY NEW IDENTITY

There comes a new way of thinking when you establish your identity with your earthly family as well as your Heavenly Father. When you know who you are, you are not going to settle for old patterns of thinking that may have been self-destructive. This can take time to establish, as you actually have to make a conscious effort not to do or act in ways that were once harmful to yourself or others.

When you begin to understand who you are, and when you no longer have to beg for what you feel you need. You can go confidently to your Heavenly Father for what your heart desires. My prayer life has indeed changed and I am learning to rest in His presence so that I can walk into new realities. When I understand who I am, I am able to draw on that deep well that is in the Father but also in me. I can also refresh others who are thirsty and are in need of knowing who they are, for now I know from my own experience what this means. This means that I can encounter others as an established child of God, a mother in the faith, and a doer of His will here on earth. I am reminded of the scripture in Ephesians 1:5. It states:

*"He predestined us to adoption
as sons through Jesus Christ to*

CHAPTER 3

I LOOK LIKE MY *Father*...NO I REALLY DO

*Himself, according to the kind
intention of his will."*

Can you imagine? We literally belong to God.
Our lives are to reflect who we are and whose we
are. As we step into our identity as sons and
daughters, and as a royal priesthood here on earth,
we become shining ones, examples of how
humanity is to live on earth. This may not be
something that you can imagine just yet, but I am
believing that God will expose all of us to who
we are to be.

It is my sincere prayer that everyone I come
into contact with will walk into this new reality
for themselves and that each person enjoys the
beautiful journey ahead in this area.

CHAPTER 4

JUST SAY *Yes*

"Sometimes the difference between the mundane and greatness is a simple yes."

JUST SAY *Yes*

Sometimes the difference between the mundane and greatness is a simple yes. Saying yes positions you for the greater in life. This has absolutely happened to me when I have said yes, especially when the conditions wouldn't have supported it.

I remember when the idea of attending Bethel School of Supernatural Ministry (BSSM) dropped into my heart. I immediately wanted to dismiss it. I said to myself "there's no way that I can uproot myself and disrupt my family, let alone to move out of the state of Alaska. I submitted the application and really didn't think much of it. Soon afterwards, I scheduled an interview and was accepted before I knew it. I was faced with having to give my two week notice and figure out, with my family, how to transition to California. Everything happened so quickly that it caught me off guard, and I truly witnessed a miracle in how everything came together. My husband and daughter would remain in Alaska and I would live in California for those nine months.

IT TAKES COURAGE TO LEAN IN

I found that it takes courage to lean in and say yes. When you say yes, it most likely means you will have to throw caution to the wind and walk outside of your comfort zone. I know that if I didn't say yes to BSSM I would always wonder about the "what if" and that nothing would really change in my life. However, if I said yes, I would experience life more abundantly.

GRACE ENABLES YOU TO
WALK IN THE IMPOSSIBLE

I'm reminded of Peter when he was in the boat on the Sea of Galilee[1]. When Peter and his friends saw Jesus walking on the water, Peter called out to the Lord, and the Lord called out to Peter, telling him to come onto the water. Peter was faced with a choice: either walk on the water to meet the Lord or stay in the boat. Instead of staying with the familiar, Peter did something he never would have dreamed of; by stepping out, and walking on the water, he said yes to the Lord.

There are many things in this life that will try and keep you from walking in the area of your MORE. The MORE is a state of being and a place within ourselves that will bring us into a greater revelation of who He is and who we are to be in the earth. You may be asking yourself, "what could that possibly mean?". Well, when Jesus died on the cross, He said YES in order for us to live as we were created to live. I will explore this in depth shortly.

YES CHANGES THINGS

When I said yes to move to Redding, I had a sense that I was in for a huge surprise and exponential change. The truth of the matter is that God will give you the strength and ability to function in what he has called you to do. This is called grace and is the divine enablement to do what you normally couldn't do on your own. Does grace mean that you escape trials in your life? Not at all, but if you can choose to lean on God, you will experience the unforced rhythms of grace. A perfect example of this in my life is that while I was in Redding, my husband was responsible for paying for the mortgage at home, the rent in Redding, and other expenses. God supplied every

---

[1] Matthew 14:22-33

single need; we even had extra to bless people around us on a consistent basis.

YOUR YES AFFECTS OTHERS

When I said yes to this transition, my daughter ended up coming to visit me. She was forever changed and she found herself coming into divine alignment with every area of her life. If you were to ask her about her experience, she may tell you that she ended up rededicating her life to God after years of being an atheist. She was no longer depressed, her body was healed from diabetes, her physical vision was restored, and a host of other things too long to list here. The biggest miracle is that she has hope for her future and she has decided to give her yes as well.

THEY SAID YES

When you look at history, it is filled with people who have said yes, and this act of obedience changed the world. There are people we can list off the top of our heads who have said yes: King David said yes, Moses said yes, Ruth and Esther said yes, the Apostles, Mother Theresa, Martin Luther King Jr., Billy Graham all said yes. To me, the most important "yes" was the one that Jesus said when He said yes to the cross. I stated earlier that I would continue to share about Jesus' yes. His yes was God's yes. This yes changed not only the lives of humanity but the lives of all who came into contact with Him. His YES made it so that hell had no more sting. His YES opened the door for you and I to have free access to the Father with no hindrances. His YES has allowed for all of humanity to engage in a process where we become whole and are not tethered by guilt, shame, and sin.

WILL YOU SAY YES?

There are countless others who have said yes
as well and have therefore changed history.
There are always people who will decide to
sell out to saying Yes and to moving with His
grace. These are the ones who you will hear
saying "there has to be more" or "I have to
have more of a move of God in my life." We
all must begin to seek the presence of God as
we will grow and be able to bring the Father
to those who do not know Him.

Will you take courage, lean in, and say
yes? There is grace for you if you decide to,
as God always makes a way when we say yes
to Him.

CHAPTER 5

THE *Truth* ABOUT

IDENTITY THEFT

"As we gain full knowledge of who we are, we can rest assured that God will lead us, protect us, fill us, and raise us up."

Have you ever watched those television commercials that offer you protection against Identity Theft? They really have you thinking, especially as you watch the actors in the commercials who are either the victims of the crime or the people who purchased the protection. The ones who have purchased the protection are secure that their identities will not be stolen and that they can maintain who they are. I have been comparing this worldly situation to a spiritual one in my own life…

What I've learned over the years is that we usually grow up imitating those who help to raise us, good or bad. Our earthly identity is found in our parents. For me, the effect of growing up in a fractured home was that I had core identity issues, which led to a self-destructive lifestyle. Even though I had my father's last name, I had no idea of what that really meant, so I never really knew my true identity.

GOING BACK TO THE FOUNDATION

What I have learned in the process of finding myself is that in order to fix the "breach in the wall," as it pertains to my identity, I have to survey my life and go back to the very beginning. I have to forgive my parents and work through issues of pain and disappointment so that I can accept the gift of God in my life. This is actually what I call healing the heart of the matter. God so loved us that he gave…we know this scripture, yet it's hard to believe that God would do such an act of love for us.

To actually grab ahold of His truth over my life would literally take an unveiling (so to speak) that would reveal to me who I am in God's eyes. The Bible says in Genesis 1:27 that God created man in His image. The scriptures also say in Luke 12:7 that every hair on my head is numbered, and in Jeremiah 17:10 it says that He knows me inside and out; God actually knows my heart. The truth of the matter is that the enemy has worked tirelessly to rob us of who we are. The devil has used various things to accomplish this. For instance, I used to use substances, I was in destructive self-sabotaging relationships, and I was full of self-hatred...all because I had no idea who I was, or who I was created to be.

ENTER IN

As we gain full knowledge of who we are, we can rest assured that God will lead us, protect us, fill us, and raise us up. I believe that King David tapped into this reality. I read the 23ʳᵈ Psalm differently now. Now I read it as an heir, a child of God. I can enter into the place of rest and know that God is my Father who will lead me and provide my every need. I can now take part in God's divine economy. My Heavenly Father withholds no good thing from me. This is God's original intention as He didn't want to ever keep goodness from Adam or Eve.

Therefore, I am reminded that as Adam and Eve were in the garden, they made choices that caused a shift as to how they saw themselves. When their identity was robbed from them, they then saw themselves through a lens that was faulty. It was devoid of the love that was given to them in the beginning. Before the fall, Adam would eagerly meet His Father, His Friend, His God with full abandon. It took Jesus dying on the cross to bring us into a space where we could freely obtain His love.

SAFE AND SOUND

If the devil can convince us that we are not worthy to be a son or daughter of God, then he will think that he has disabled us. The enemy doesn't want us to walk in our authority. Our true identity can be found in God; therefore, everything pertaining to me is kept safe and sound. I'm now aware when the enemy is trying to steal my identity and I can now stop it before it happens. I have tapped into divine protection and I have agreed with my Creator about my life and who I am. I believe this is why it is so important that there are mothers and fathers in the spirit so that they can help to raise spiritual sons and daughters. These sons and daughters can then grow and mature to see who they really are and that they will walk in dominion over the land. These sons and daughters will then be able to release the Kingdom of God here on earth. I believe that this is what God has intended for us to do. He desires that we release the kingdom here on the earth and that we lead others in doing the same thing.

ASK AND IT WILL BE GIVEN

We have to actually ask our Creator who we are and who we were created to be. As we settle into who we are and allow ourselves to abide in Him, He will abide in us (John 15:7). To *abide*[1] actually means to continue in a particular condition, attitude, or relationship (Dictionary.com). This is a verb which means it is in continual action. It is a movement and it must be stewarded.

When we engage the presence of God, we actually begin to participate in a divine exchange. That exchange helps us to see ourselves beyond what our human experiences can comprehend. To walk in your authentic identity is actually the high calling you were meant to operate in and possess. It's higher than any particular gifting or ability. This is you walking in your divine status as a son or daughter of the Most High God.

The devil likes to keep us busy by preoccupying us with how we perceive ourselves.

---

1 ""Abide." Dictionary.com. Unabridged, based on the Random House Dictionary, © Random House, Inc. 2018.

Accessed September 2,2016. www.dictionary.com/browse/abide

We end up comparing ourselves with others, being envious, self-promoting, antagonistic, or depressed because we don't feel that God favors us. WOW! To think all of those lies are stomped out as we step into the truth of who we are! The devil knows that as soon as you walk into your true identity, you will be unstoppable to him. In Matthew 4:1-11, Satan approached Jesus when Jesus came off of a forty day fast. Satan thought he could confuse Jesus and speak to His flesh by trying to tempt Him in His identity. However, Jesus knew who He was and that He had already (key word) defeated the devil. Because of that, Jesus did not sell His inheritance. As a result, we are all now partakers in this glorious inheritance. Did you notice that after Jesus was firm in His identity as the Son of God, he began his ministry? The same goes for us.

KEEPING OUR INHERITANCE

I've started to compare the parable of the Prodigal Son to when we are not operating in our true identity. When we choose not to step into our true identity, but choose self-sabotage (strife, self-pity, and the like), we are selling our inheritance only to sleep in the pig pen. But like the Prodigal Son, we can stand up, dust ourselves off, and determine to go back to our loving Father's embrace. It is then that we begin to understand what it meant when the Prodigal Son "came to his senses" as we turn our affections towards the Father.

Let's decide to protect our identity. Let's agree with Heaven about who God says we are. Let's decide to enter into Him and release this truth over the earth. As we decide to do this, we will then begin to shine as the children of light that we are. We will begin to shine forth as we have been called to do.

CHAPTER 6

ENTER INTO HIS *Rest*.

*"For me to enter into rest
means that I must cast off any
anxiety, any fear, or anything
that will take me away from
the knowledge and presence
of God ...."*

CHAPTER 6

ENTER INTO HIS *Rest*

ENTERING INTO A SEASON OF REST

There is always a time, around the holidays, when it seems that we get caught up in the hustle and bustle of the season. It seems inevitable that through this stress we lose our sense of peace and calm. Even though we hear people say that Jesus is the reason for the season, the reality of that feels far from our situations.

For the last six months or so I have been on a journey learning about God's rest and how to enter in to this state of being. The idea of rest is everywhere. We search for the best mattresses and watch commercials where people search high and low for a comfortable and restful night's sleep. The concept of rest is ideally put above almost anything else.

REST IS A GIFT

Rest is not something to be earned. In the scriptures, Jesus said that He will GIVE us rest. With that being said, we often find ourselves laboring in order to rest. What does this look like? For me to enter into rest means that I must cast off any anxiety, any fear, or anything that will take me away from the knowledge and presence of God as the Lord of my life. I remember when I first heard this concept. It was a little confusing to me as I looked at labor as job or work related. As a result, I would equate rest with something that was earned (just like earning vacation time at work). However, rest is something you will enter into, and something that is given to you. The only action that is required is that we ENTER into it.

PSALM 23

When reading the 23rd Psalm, we see how David entered into rest with His Heavenly Father. David was able to tap into rest as he had a revelation of this concept. Let's look at the following verses:

Psalm 23

*1 The LORD is my shepherd; I shall not want.
2 He makes me lie down in green pastures; He leads me beside quite waters.
3 He restores my soul; He guides me in the paths of righteousness for His name's sake.*

When we allow the Lord to be our shepherd, it means that we allow Him to lead and guide us. This means that we do not have to have anxiety about what is to come, because we are guided and led by the One who cares for our every need.

We have been invited to come and lie down in green pastures. Taking the invitation means that we are fed and cared for by the Good Shepherd; God sees to it that we are led strategically by His hand to a place of peace and tranquility. This is participation in God's Divine economy. Such a divine economy means that we tap into His grace, even when chaos is swirling around us and we cannot figure out why. It gives us the certainty that we will be led to green pastures and beside still waters.

The result is that He will restore our souls. He will nourish and redeem that which has been shaken or questioned. According to Dictionary.com, to *restore* means to bring back to a state of soundness, health, or vigor; to put back to a former position, rank or to reproduce or

ENTER INTO HIS *Rest*.

reconstruct in the original state. When I read this definition, I thought of Adam and his place in the Garden of Eden. Adam was in a constant place of rest when he was in the garden. He was in constant communion with God and God was in communion with him. Unfortunately, when the fall of man happened, we lost our original state of rest and entered into toil and turmoil. But Jesus, and His sacrifice on the cross, opened the door for us to enter a place of rest and oneness with God again.

DIVINE ORDER

We begin to operate in divine order when we enter His rest. When we cast all of our cares upon the Lord, He in turn will lead us beside still waters. To operate in divine order is to give Him lordship over our lives. What that looks like for me is to not be consumed with worry over money, over what will happen tomorrow or the next day.

To give Him lordship means that I lay everything down at the cross and then I pick up joy and gladness in its place. Sometimes, I have to do a physical activity to demonstrate this truth in my life. I sometimes will sit down in a chair and take a deep breath. It reminds me of the scripture that states that we are seated with Him in heavenly places (Ephesians 2:6). That verse doesn't say that we pace around the room wringing our hands in heavenly places, it states that we are SEATED with HIM in heavenly places. This is what brings the divine order into our lives, which then allows us to see the bigger picture--the picture from the eagle's eye view; the view from above the fray.

REST WILL ALWAYS BRING
DOMINION OVER CHAOS

In Matthew 11, Jesus says "*Come to Me, all who are weary and heavy laden, and I will give you rest.*" In the rest of this passage, Jesus describes the yoke that is waiting for us. Instead of a yoke of heaviness and burdens, we take upon ourselves His yoke and Jesus states that "*you will find rest for your SOULS.*" This takes me back to how God will restore our souls as we allow Him to lead us beside still waters and green pastures.

Recently I had a situation where there was chaos in my life that tried to shake my peace. Through practice and being intentional, I did not find myself being taken under by the chaos. Instead I was able to speak to chaos and the "storm" disappeared. This is a lesson that I have learned by reading about how Jesus could sleep during the storm on the sea. While the chaos of the storm raged on, and the others feared the waves of the sea, Jesus spoke to the storm and the chaos ended (Matthew 8:24).

THE PROCESS CONTINUES

As we learn how to labor into His rest, we realize that this is a process that we must engage and practice often. This isn't something that we will do only when it's convenient. It is something that we must do on a regular basis. It is out of rest that we allow the refining process to do its full work. This is the refining process that shows me how the wounds of my heart have been filled with gold.

CHAPTER 7

LIVING AN

Unveiled LIFE

"...it is the time for me to live an unveiled life. A life full of beauty and passion while being my authentic self --the self that desires the fullness of God."

Have you ever thought about how we sometimes feel we must be all things to all people? It is true. Even if you feel that you aren't doing it, there are times when we act differently in front of friends than we do in front of those we live and work with. I know that I have worked very hard to make sure that I am authentic in all areas of my life. When I think of living unveiled, I think of being unafraid to be my true self. I think of not being intimidated by my own lack or shortcomings. To be myself means that I can rest assured in my identity because I know who I am.

LETTING THE PAST HURTS GO
TO BE FREE TODAY

When you are willing to let go of the residue of past pains, you create an opportunity for God to do more in your life. You are allowing yourself to encounter God as your Creator, in a deeper, more meaningful way.

I have found this principle at work in my own life. Let me explain. When I was growing up, I was exposed to situations that created a unique challenge that sometimes would cause me to become stagnant or to retreat into my own world of judgment. These areas would hinder me from being my authentic self because, I felt that other people saw me the way I saw myself through the same lens of shame, guilt, worry, etc.

As I entered a loving relationship with my Savior, I slowly began to realize that over time, I could lift the veil of shame, guilt, self-hatred, and pain, and enter into a full relationship with my Creator. Lifting this veil helped me to see clearly. Each time I would remove a veil that clouded my vision, no matter what it was, I came into a fuller, more genuine relationship with God as my Father.

Just imagine trying to look through a thick veil to see where you are going. It is not easy unless someone is guiding you. I think of how

LIVING AN *Unveiled* LIFE

when a bride is walking down the aisle, her face is covered with a veil, and she is guided by her father or the person she has elected to present her to her groom. This is the same case when we are standing before our heavenly Father. If we are veiled, we cannot see His face clearly. We will always see Him through distortions such as shame, guilt, etc. I have also noticed, in my own life, that the veils that concealed my authentic self were the ones that keep me bound to the past.

UNVEILED AND FREE

This statement means a lot to me as I am currently coming into an understanding of what it means to live unveiled and free. I know that I am living unveiled because I can respond, instead of reacting, to certain situations.

An example is someone who feels ashamed to share their life with people. This person could be seeing him or herself through a veil that would cause a sense of being unworthy of relationships and friendships.

The veils that we wear will keep us from seeing ourselves as loved and adored because we will always see ourselves as unworthy. This realization has caused me to think about how attached I have become to the veils that have been used to hide my identity.

OUR TRUE SELVES

I have thought about how wonderful it would be to be able to walk in my authentic and true self. This requires me to understand the sacrifice that was paid for me and my freedom. I have to consciously decide to partner with the God of hope in order to move forward. This means that I have to grow comfortable in my own skin as I allow myself to remove the veil that covers my identity. This will allow me to be myself with those that I know well, and with those I am just getting to know.

I want to be one hundred percent real with everyone that I meet, and especially with myself. For that to be possible I will need to take chances and let the "chips fall where they may". Does this mean that I act any old kind of way, or that I am rude or obnoxious? Absolutely not! Instead I will be kind just as my true and authentic self is on a regular basis.

FINALLY UNVEILED

But we all, with unveiled face,
beholding as in a mirror
The glory of the Lord, are being
transformed into the same
From glory to glory, just as
from the Lord, the Spirit. II
Corinthians 3:18 NASB

As I make my journey through my second year at Bethel School of Supernatural Ministry (BSSM), I am understanding what it means to be free and unveiled. I don't make decisions based on hurts or pains from the past. I want to see the face of God in those situations, so I allow myself time to reflect and sit with the emotions that are surfacing. This is the process of allowing the hooks from the past and the hooks that would keep me bound here on earth to be let go of. I really do believe that it is the time for me to live an unveiled life a life full of beauty and passion while being my authentic self --the self that desires the fullness of God.

CHAPTER 7
LIVING AN *Unveiled* LIFE

GOING FORWARD

It is my prayer that you live your life unveiled that you walk unobstructed and free, and then nothing from your past holds you back, ever. I pray you can turn towards your Creator unashamed. I would also love to hear how you can identify the various veils (if any) that are in your life, and how you can live your life free!

CHAPTER 8

Arise AND Shine

"For me to become
illuminated would mean that
I would shine forth in this
world, so consumed with His
love that when you looked at
me, you would see only
Him."

Arise AND Shine

SHINE BRIGHT

To read the words "Arise and Shine," I'm reminded of how we were made to shine and to illuminate. I have recently begun to uncover the concept that I truly am a carrier of His light. We sing the songs "This Little Light of Mine" but I didn't have a true revelation of the meaning until recently. It happened in November 2016 when I was at a meeting where we discussed being in the image of our Creator in our hearts, minds, and souls. I know that Jesus has a place in my heart, but I really didn't understand how He causes us to become illuminated with His love and care.

For me to become illuminated would mean that I would shine forth in this world, so consumed with His love that when you looked at me, you would see only Him. This has a daily process of transformation, and I do mean daily. There are days that, when I wake up, I have to remind myself that I am being transformed and molded into the person I was meant to be.

I remember being at a meeting where I began to see in my mind's eye a future version of what I looked like. I literally saw myself as a woman carrying light in my hands, with light coming from body. This image of me carrying the light automatically took me to the Parable of the 10 Virgins in Matthew 25:1-13:

> *At that time the kingdom of heaven will be like ten virgins who took their lamps and went out to meet the bridegroom. Five of them were foolish and five were wise. The foolish ones took their lamps but did not take any oil with them. The wise ones, however, took oil in jars*

along with their lamps. The bridegroom was a long time in coming, and they all became drowsy and fell asleep. "At midnight the cry rang out: 'Here's the bridegroom! Come out to meet him!' "Then all the virgins woke up and trimmed their lamps. The foolish ones said to the wise, 'Give us some of your oil; our lamps are going out.' "'No,' they replied, 'there may not be enough for both us and you. Instead, go to those who sell oil and buy some for yourselves.' "But while they were on their way to buy the oil, the bridegroom arrived. The virgins who were ready went in with him to the wedding banquet. And the door was shut. "Later the others also came. 'Lord, Lord,' they said, 'open the door for us!' "But he replied, 'Truly I tell you, I don't know you.' "Therefore, keep watch, because you do not know the day or the hour."

When we see that five of the virgins had oil with them, and that these five were considered wise, it helps us to understand that in a practical sense we should ensure we that always have oil with us and that we are prepared. But after I had this vision of my future self, God showed me that I was a light bearer. The oil should always be used to keep the flame burning, since the oil represents the Holy Spirit and the flame represents His light that dwells within us.

We are the ones who are responsible for carrying Him and having Him as our light to shine in the darkness. We need the constant oil of the Holy Spirit to fill us up. If we don't keep filled,

Arise AND *Shine*

we run the risk of not being as a light unto all the earth. In this parable the Father is communicating about Christ being the Bridegroom. The five virgins with the lamps but no oil were the ones that were preoccupied with their own issues as opposed to being focused on the Father's business.

I believe that our Creator is wanting us to live the life we were supposed to live before the fall of man happened. We are the ones that are supposed to bear His image. We carry His breath in our lungs and can live a life full of abundance and hope.

When I heard the word arise, it speaks of waking up from slumber and taking off the "grave clothes," so to speak. To arise means to be fully me all the time --to be free to be authentic in all areas and situations.

The enemy has made it a mission that we remain asleep, unaware of who we are and what our purpose is. Teresa of Avila, a 16th century nun, stated, "The chief duty of man is to glorify God and enjoy Him forever." The enemy of our soul desires to keep us from being able to see God for who He is. If we can find a reason to not lean into Him, to not enjoy Him, then our flesh will build up our walls of self-protection and we will end up keeping Him out. What I have found is that God is never distant from me. It is always me who is distant from Him, and I am the one who causes the separation to happen.

In the Garden of Eden, Satan's strategy was to bring doubt and to sow shame and guilt with the end goal being separation between God and man. This was never supposed to be the plan and these things were never supposed to be part of our identity. The enemy knew this and has worked to try and entangle us in a web of lies. God made Adam and Eve with the intention that they would live forever with Him. Death was never supposed to be in the plan. The enemy perverted what God had stated to man and from that moment on, mankind was ensnared. It took the coming of the "second Adam", Jesus, to live as a sacrifice to redeem man's life.

IT'S TIME TO RISE

God is waking up humanity so that we can walk into our destiny here on earth. When we open our eyes and allow our hearts to come alive to His love and care, we can then begin to move in Him and walk in our true identity. It is this process of uncovering and unveiling that allows us to be able to look into a mirror with full confidence that we are children of God and that we are filled with light and grace.

As long as we find ourselves struggling with the familiar lies of the enemy shame, guilt, rejection, and other self-destructive ideas or behaviors, we will remain out of alignment until we unveil that part of our heart that needs healing. We will always have contention growing in our hearts and minds as long as we continue to embrace Satan's lies as part of our identity. (the fruit from the tree of knowledge of good and evil). This fruit will only yield death and there is no life in it. But if we eat from the tree of life we can still embrace hope and a future not only ourselves but for those around us who are directly impacted by our lives.

In my second year of ministry school, I came face to face with a part of my heart that was growing and fostering a lie. It shook me and caused me to really examine myself in order to pull out this weed or "tare" that was growing alongside all of the positive things I was embracing about my identity. When I think of this memory, I think of the story in the Bible where Jesus tells the parable of the wheat and the tares (Matthew 13:24-30) and how the both of them will grow up together. There will be a time, though, when you can tell them apart and when that happens, you can uproot the tare and throw it into the fire. I remember one day in class when our speaker, Pastor Kris Vallotton, described that when the wheat was fully mature, it would bow down, but the tare would remain straight. Imagine that, when the fruit of your life becomes mature, it will cause you to bow, to become humble as opposed to the "junk" or weeds which will erect themselves and make themselves known. That is how rejection, or any other fruit of the flesh will respond. Rejection will not yield to God or His way and will make itself resistant to the love of God. An interesting thing about this parable is that the tares have to be thrown into the fire. This would mean that we have to cast the tares (shame, guilt, rejection, etc.) away, not cast God or our true selves away.

We were made to shine, loved ones. We were meant to live a life of fulfillment, not a life hindered by what we perceive as our shortcomings. It truly is our time to Rise and Shine!

CHAPTER 9

THE *Beauty*

IN RESISTANCE

"…there is a key to be gained in engaging the resistance, a key to overcoming and a key to a victorious life."

THE *Beauty* IN RESISTANCE

Recently, I have been thinking of the multiple times that I have felt resistance or experienced it. It is certainly not my favorite feeling, but there is a purpose in it. Most of the time when we feel resistance, we will either retreat or we will forge forward. I believe that there is a key to be gained in engaging the resistance a key to overcoming and a key to a victorious life.

I believe that resistance can and will most likely show up in an area where we face difficulty in trusting in the Lord. For me this was in finances. There was a time when I would panic if I had to place all my trust in God in this area and I felt like I was on my own. I could believe in miracles for everyone around me, but when it pertained to miracles for myself, I couldn't believe or fully trust God. I think this is because I didn't see myself as worthy as a daughter of the Creator. When I remarried my husband (yes remarried), I could feel that a change was beginning to happen and that a place of ease was created. I finally felt freedom from my past of poverty-stricken memories and that I was beginning to feel victory over the trauma of lack.

Yet even though I was remarried, I still had an area of my life that I didn't fully release for complete healing. This area shone brightly through much pressure and I would soon need an encounter with the presence of God to shift my perspective of who I was becoming.

In my second year of ministry school, I was presented with ministry opportunities (like all second-year students). There were two opportunities that I felt like God was leading me to. One was Argentina and the other Asia. Mind you, I had my daughter's ministry trip to Sierra Leone to raise money for as well, which was very expensive. At this point, I could stand in my own strength and knowledge, but I began to see how much I needed a deeper revelation of God's goodness and grace.

I remember as I was coming up on a hard deadline for my Asia ministry trip, I began to tell God I don't know how this would ever happen, but You do. I would sometimes be awakened at night with fear or with anxiety as to how this would happen. This was resistance for me as this was pushing on the buttons that triggered my past pain in this area of provision. At that moment, I could either lean into the resistance and go where the Spirit was leading me or I could retreat back into what was familiar, which in this case was trusting myself over my Father. One day during this process, my husband called and said "Babe, we don't have the extra money to give for any ministry trips. You will have to let them know that you can't go." Even though this was extremely practical, I couldn't just "let it go". I told him that I wanted to wait before I pulled out of the ministry trip all together because I was just given an extension of a couple of days. This was on a Thursday and on a Friday evening, I received an unexpected call from a dear friend in Alaska. She stated that the Holy Spirit placed me on her heart approximately five different times that day and that she knew that she had to call me. We talked about school and upcoming events and then she stated that she wanted to give me $1000 towards my ministry trip to Asia. Even now when I think of this, I become overwhelmed by the goodness of God. It is truly amazing how God meets our needs, wants, and desires.

Shortly after the Asia miracle, I was granted another financial breakthrough by a stranger at a restaurant. It was a Sunday morning after church and me a friend from ministry school decided to go and have a late breakfast at Madayne's a restaurant in Redding, California. As we sat down to eat, a gentleman came up to me and stated that he would like to give me a word of encouragement. He stated that I would soon experience a financial breakthrough and that I would see how faithful God is to me. I thanked him and told him that I was praying for provision

CHAPTER 9

THE *Beauty* IN RESISTANCE

for an upcoming ministry trip to South America
and how this was such a great word of
encouragement. The gentleman and his wife soon
left the restaurant and my friend and I continued
to eat and after a while we left to go on with our
day. About 2 hours later, I had to pick up my
daughter from her church service. When I picked
her up, she stated that she was hungry and wanted
to go to Madayne's. I said, "No way, I was just
there and this will look weird". We went there
anyway and there was the same gentleman who
had given me a word of encouragement a few
hours earlier. We made eye contact and I
continued to walk to the counter to order my
daughter's food. As I proceeded back to the table,
the gentleman came right up to me and told me
that the Holy Spirit was leading him to give me
money for my trip but that he didn't have it earlier
when he saw me. He then he said something that
blew me away. He stated, "I told the Lord that if
I see this woman again today, before I leave
California, then I know I am supposed to give her
money for her ministry trip to Argentina". I was
absolutely in shock at how everything was
coming together. The gentleman and his wife
brought me to their table, pulled out their credit
card and paid my trip in full (which was $1000).
I look at these two situations and see them as
answers to prayer of course, but I also see this as
a way to take and gain new territory in my heart.

When I was a single parent, the pressure of not
making enough and not having enough, made me
feel as though I wanted to retreat. The best way I
can explain how I felt was that it almost felt that
God was not going to provide. But God always
did and always will. Basically, what I am saying
is that when thoughts creep up in our lives that
remind us of past emotional trauma, difficult
situations or just painful times, those memories
will present as resistance. It is up to us to push
through the resistance and walk out on the other

side of the pain.

THE JOURNEY TO TRUST

Trusting God in these times almost feels like walking blindfolded with only His voice to guide you. You can't see and sometimes you don't know what is ahead of you, but this is the time that we should lean in and begin to trust Him. The way that this will look, as it pertains to resistance, is to basically say "Lord, I trust and believe you." When you make this statement, you are stating that you are choosing to rest in Him and not lean on your own understanding. This will begin the journey in entering His rest. Trust and rest go hand in hand and I have found that when I decide to trust in His nature and not my own, I can think clearly, believe in His ways, and then I feel victorious in whatever mountain I am trying to climb.

In the journey to trust, it will require us to see life and our circumstances through new lenses. I was speaking to a fellow business owner today who was having a difficult time and was facing resistance to make the necessary changes in her life to see success. Because I know her well, I know the challenges she has faced in the past and how she is trying to achieve breakthrough. When I spoke with her about her circumstances and what she was going to do to push through, she stated that she initially felt as if she wanted to run from the issues that were surfacing. As we talked, she began to recognize a pattern of pain that would always have her retreat, it was as if she had an "ah hah" moment. I firmly believe that resistance can sometimes be an indicator that you may disrupt a pattern of behavior that has kept you from moving forward. When we decide to disengage the distractions (patterns, triggers, etc.) then this is when we will make the changes necessary that will affect our lives and our quality of life.

CHAPTER 9
THE *Beauty* IN RESISTANCE

We can also see resistance in nature as well. Look at creation and how everything that births the "new" faces resistance. The seedlings that are planted in the earth push through the soil to sprout. The baby birds break through their shells to be birthed. The examples could go on and on (like people changing addictive behaviors, etc.) but you understand the point. If we start seeing our circumstances and the role that they play in our lives differently, we could begin to walk in our true authority.

In reading Ezra Chapter 4, we see how the Jews who were in exile were granted the ability to leave and rebuild in Israel. As the people were building the temple, resistance came to them in the form of threats, intimidation, confusion, and discouragement. This was difficult for those that were rebuilding as this posed a distraction. Although the Jews were on assignment from God to rebuild, they still faced resistance in the form of opposition. May I suggest that when we feel confusion, discouragement, and threats against who we are as sons and daughters, that it could be the enemy of our soul? Could it be that the enemy is trying to keep us from where we are supposed to be going, and keeping us from fulfilling our assignment here on earth, and from shining forth as God intended?

All of this to say that we are to be mindful of the things that will bring resistance in our lives. As we see resistance with a new perspective, we can then embrace the change that we are to step into and become the picture of who we are supposed to be. The next time you sense resistance, try and discern where it is coming from, what you are supposed to learn from it and how you are to grow as a result.

CHAPTER 10

BECAUSE HE IS *Faithful*

> "Knowing that He is Faithful
> is paramount for us as we
> journey into who we are
> called to be."

CHAPTER 10
BECAUSE HE IS *Faithful*

As I have grown and have had some experience with the Creator, I have come to know Him as faithful. There are many times when a challenging situation happened, yet, He always proved to be faithful. It reminds me of how when I was growing up, I would hear older people say "my word is my bond.". This is how God is with us. Even if we cannot say that our word is our bond, His word is always sure, tried and true. There are certain times within my life that I have been challenged through circumstances. During these times, I would cry out to God (literally) for help. There was a sense of incredible agony when I would cry to Him. The part of my life where I needed to be in His grace the most was in the area of finances. This is where I began to see His faithfulness come forward.

Growing up with lack seemed to have made a mark on my life. This was evident by the deep sorrow I would feel, especially as I would have to depend on God to help me to make ends meet. Although my mother was a very hard worker, there were times that all of her efforts would not be enough. My mother didn't have a steady community, nor did she have anything to anchor herself to when times were lean. This would mean that any type of hope or faith she would have would fluctuate with her feelings.

I must admit that I never really understood anything as it pertained to finances when I was a child. I understood that I received school lunch and that we couldn't eat out that often, but I never knew my mother's endless nights of crying and anguish raising a child on her own. The effects of this did play out in my adult life, however, as I became a single parent myself and lack would stare me in the face. It wasn't until I became reconciled with my heavenly Father that I began to understand how faithful he truly was. Allow me to explain.

After my mother passed away, I had found

myself with my feelings really hurt. I was hurt because my mom wasn't religious and therefore unable to reconcile the hardships in her life. So when her life ended, I found myself tired and alone, but I then began to feel a draw, a yearning and a pull towards God that was undeniable. This all happened as I watched a Billy Graham Crusade on television in September 1995.

HE IS FAITHFUL WHEN WE ARE FAITHLESS

If we are faithless, He remains faithful, for He cannot deny Himself. **(II Timothy 2:13)**

There was something that stirred in my spirit that rose up and said "I want to believe". I believe that on that day when I said "yes" to believing in His goodness, I was radically changed. That was September 1995. I like to tell this part of my story because God is completely capable of understanding where we are and what we need at any particular time in our lives. HE IS GOOD AND IS INCAPABLE OF ANYTHING ELSE.

When I think of trusting in God, I am reminded of little baby chicks who follow their momma around. They have no idea where she is bringing them, or what she will do next. They just follow. All they know is that their momma is their shelter, their protector and they love her. She will call them to her and they will gather around her and she will then cover them with her wings.

This is what God desires to do with us. He desires for us to trust Him and to follow Him implicitly. He is a good Father who means no harm to His children. I'm reminded of two scriptures. One is Psalm 91 in which David states with full assurance (this has to be from his own personal experience) that He (God) will cover you. It states:

CHAPTER 10

BECAUSE HE IS *Faithful*

He will cover you with His
feathers and
under His wings you will find
refuge;
His faithfulness will be your
shield and rampart. **(Psalms**
91:4)

Can you see how His faithfulness towards us is something that will remain...even when we are faithless?

There is a time where we can refuse to be "gathered together" and brought under His shelter. This is the example in Matthew 23:37:

Jerusalem, Jerusalem, you who
kill the prophets and stone those
sent to you, how often I have
longed to gather your children
together, as a hen gathers her
chicks under her wings, and you
were not willing.

His desire is to be our covering, but I remember a time when it was hard for me to come under His covering and to be gathered unto Him. The one thing that I have learned over the years, is that He does not want to be anything less than a gentleman. He will not force Himself onto you, as He wants everything to be your choice.

Through this process, I have learned, that if I am carrying stuff that prevents me from entering into His presence and understanding His faithfulness, then I must do what I can to free myself from myself. I have to be diligent in untethering myself from my doubts, worrying and anxieties. All that and the like are a false reality. It is not where we are to be living and breathing and the enemy of our souls understands that. This is why the battle to remain untethered IS REAL.

UNTETHERED

As we become untethered to doubt, fear, anxiety, anger, etc., we will then be free to become attached to the Father and only Him. There are only a few things that can keep us from being held close to Him. It all stems from our perspective of how we see Him responding to us. I have found that it literally takes a type of boldness for us to move past the "junk" that gets in or way. It just takes an encounter with our Heavenly Father in order for us to be set free from all of this. But once we become free, we are free indeed! The freedom we can experience will allow us to delve into who He is and His nature. Knowing that He is Faithful is paramount for us as we journey into who we are called to be.

While I was in second year at BSSM, I had an experience with His faithfulness. I was setting a session towards the end of the year where the Revival Group Pastors who mentored us all year took turns speaking to our hearts in what was to be called Staff Speaking Week. The pastor that I chose was speaking that day on God's faithfulness. She encouraged us to press in when we were in prayer and to concentrate on His faithfulness.

As we began to pray, I instantly went into an encounter where all I saw was this very large field. It looked as though it was a field for crops but there wasn't anything growing nor was there anything green. Then the heavens opened up, lightening cracked and an abundance of rain began to fall onto the dry land. Then I heard His voice say, "It's because I'm faithful". Then just like a scene in a movie, it switched to a nest with four baby birds awaiting their mother's return. The baby birds all had their mouths opened and they were hungry. I began to feel deep emotion for them and their needs. Suddenly, she returned and began to feed each one of her babies. Again, I heard Him say, "It's because I'm faithful". The

CHAPTER 10

BECAUSE HE IS *Faithful*

last scene that I saw was a mother holding her little baby. The mother held and caressed the baby's face and hands. The baby looked at the mother with complete love. It was as if I were sharing a sacred moment, a moment designed only to allow the human soul to flourish. Watching this flooded my own soul with such love and kindness that I became overwhelmed. Again, He said, "It's because I'm faithful".

The Lord showed me that as the fields needed rain, He sent the rain. It is not because the crops knew that they needed to be watered or that they knew they needed the rain. God knew and He then caused the crops to grow and flourish. The baby birds had a need and God knew that their need would be met by their mother coming to feed them. The mother holding her baby is an example that I think that we can all relate to. The baby trusted that the mother would not cause harm and would only love and care for her child. We are all like the baby and the mother represents our Creator and provider. The love and tenderness is a demonstration of His faithfulness and love. It is innate and it is certain.

WHAT DOES IT ALL MEAN?

In looking at all of creation and the ways that God provides His faithfulness in each and every way, it speaks to His very essence as a Father and a rock. It says to us who He really is, and that is the Faithful one. He has not changed nor will He ever change. Indeed, He cannot change.

"I am the Lord, and I change not..." **Malachi 3:6.**

Each time we are called upon to depend in His faithfulness, we are then made to make a decision. Will we lean into Him and believe Him for His faithfulness? If we choose not to lean into His faithfulness and goodness, we are choosing to lean unto our own understanding, to remain grafted into the tree of knowledge of good and evil. This is the same tree that the serpent led Eve to eat from in the garden. BUT, when we make a CHOICE to trust in His faithfulness, we feast on the tree of LIFE and expand our capacity to understand who He is and what He is doing in the Kingdom. We step into the knowledge of what Adam knew before the fall.

We were created to enjoy God and His goodness. He desires for our hearts to no longer be divided but to be one. He is calling us back to a place of love and faithfulness. That is His desire and His will for our lives here on earth.

CHAPTER 11

TRUE *North*

"My true north had been proven
to me to be the very thing that
was to keep me grounded, stable
in light of any storm that was
around me."

In my forty plus years on earth, I have searched various places for a true place in my heart to call home. This is where, for me, true north has a deep meaning. When I look up the meaning of True North, it states the following:

Noun- **North**[1] that is calculated by using an imaginary line through the Earth rather than by using a compass: the direction that leads to the North Pole.

This seems to have a very specific meaning to me especially as I have moved forward in my life in different areas. One particular area that I think that matches this is in the area of staying connected to God no matter what I walk through. This even means that if I am facing a difficult time or a time where it feels like I'm in a battle, that my true north will keep me grounded.

What I have been learning in this season in my life, is that it's about navigating the condition of your heart. This only really works if you are willing to anchor yourself to His heart and to His ways. To choose to take on emotions or thoughts that steer me away from who He is, is counterproductive and will lead me into a place of misunderstanding and to a place of distraction. Let me explain. When I was getting my daughter settled for ministry school, there were a series of events that seemed to happen all at the same time. Not one event that happened on its own, was exactly bad, but when they all fell behind each other it caused such a distraction that I actually began to focus on myself and my hurt feelings. If I am honest with myself, this is an indication of what remains in my soul that needs to be healed and dealt with. I believe that we are always on a quest to find healing and wholeness. No matter what type of condition you are in, you will always

1 "North." Dictionary.com. *The American Heritage® Idioms Dictionary*

Copyright © 2002, 2001, 1995 by Houghton Mifflin Company. Published by Houghton Mifflin Company. Accessed August 30. 2017. www.dictionary.com/browse/find-true-north

find ways to improve and evolve into the person you were destined and called to be.

With this process, something that I learned about my heart is that there is no room to hold onto anything that is not from Him. If there are emotions and past traumatic experiences that I have not surrendered to my Creator, then I have given those experiences a place to remain and a place to dwell. If I want to make sure that I am walking a life of fulfillment, then I know I have to let go of having right to use those moments from memories as self-defense/coping mechanisms. This literally brings me to the scripture in Proverbs 3:5-6:

> *Trust in the LORD with all your heart and lean not on your own understanding. In all your ways acknowledge Him and He will make your paths straight.*

What this means to me is that I won't trust the feelings of abandonment, the feelings of loneliness, the feelings of fear, anger or anything that turns me away from His heart and loving gaze. This scripture reference is full of promise for us as we decide to trust (and trust is the operative word) in Him. Trusting in Him is something that Adam and Eve did in the Garden before the fall. They trusted implicitly in God and they had no shame in who they were. They knew that they were to tend the Garden, to meet with the Creator in the cool of the day, and that they were to relate to one another in a way that demonstrated the Father's love for all of creation.

It wasn't until the serpent approached Eve and tricked her into believing that God's word wasn't enough. It sounds like something the enemy of our souls continues to do as he knows that if he can distract us from the TRUTH, then we are taken on a detour from knowing His faithfulness. I recently had a situation where I had one thing after the other that seemed to throw me off. I know that I can usually stand my ground when one obstacle happens as I am not easily detoured, but when three things, back to back in one day all happened, I was shaken. It felt as though I was kicked in the gut (for lack of a better term) and that I couldn't catch my breath.

It wasn't until later the next day that I had gained revelation of what had happened. I am someone's prayer covering back home and I knew that I was to be praying intentionally and very focused on some very specific areas. When the "hits" came at me, they caused a distraction. I wasn't thinking of God's goodness for the person I was covering, I was thinking of myself. Just what the enemy did with Eve in the garden and what he continues to do today. Once I realized that I was being duped, and when I realized what was happening, although very real, was not my true north. My true north had been proven to me to be the very thing that was to keep me grounded, stable in light of any storm that was around me.

There are times when we must push through the feelings of fear and anxiety and the unknown to obtain the truth of the Father and of who He is. The truth of the matter is that when we face times that make us feel alone, or that make us feel pain in our hearts, this is what will bring us deeper into His heart. We will find ourselves in a place of love and passion for the things that are important and for the things that will help us to rise to the place we belong...this is where the eagles soar, where the view is free from obstruction and where we can hold on to what the Father has for us.

I remember in late 2015, I had a dream where I was encountered by the love of the Father which ended up changing my whole life. In this encounter, I remember walking into a beautiful garden where there where honey bees, flowers, lush green plants, and shrubs. When I walked

TRUE North

along a path, I felt as though I wasn't alone and in fact that I was to meet the Father there to spend time with Him. All of a sudden, I began to feel such a presence of love and acceptance that I began to weep. Just at that moment, I felt my heart being drawn to this place that was far off. As I looked up and I saw rolling hills and green pastures, I heard in my spirit, "All of this is yours". I looked as far as I could see and there was a beautiful tree that was full of fruit and by a river. There was a sensation in my heart that I needed to go and sit under the tree. Just as I had thought about it, I immediately found myself there under the tree. I felt as though God wanted to hold my hand and just sit with me. I was more than happy by this point to hold His hand as this made me feel centered, grounded and I felt as though I was in a place where God wanted to pour into me as His friend.

When we allow ourselves to enter into the invitation of His kindness and love, we are then taken into a place of true identity, true oneness and we are then able to be in convergence with the one whom our soul desires.

EPILOGUE

LOVE, LIFE, AND *Beyond*

*"You will make known to me
the path of life in Your
presence is fullness of joy; In
Your right hand there are
pleasures forever."*

LOVE, LIFE, AND *Beyond*

There is always so much to consider when working towards becoming free emotionally and spiritually. When we are walking towards freedom, there has to be a place where we actually find ourselves so in love with the Father that nothing else matters. That we are completely surrounded by His love and compassion. There is no time to waste on the things that keep us bound in fear, anxiety or that keep us in toil.

Can you believe that we actually have an opportunity to move into the fullness of His Joy and to move in a manner that keeps Him as an active participant of our lives? It wasn't easy to come up with this title as I had already had a download for the sub title. But to see the vision for the main title, that was a struggle. I eventually found this title in Psalm 16 in which this has been my life verse for several years. The end of Psalm 16 states:

You will make known to me the
path of life in Your presence is
fullness of joy;
In Your right hand there are
pleasures forever.

The only way I was able to see that I had access to Joy and the fullness thereof was to have the wounds of my heart filled with the gold from God. This is when I understood that the wounds of my heart had a chance to heal and to become a place of peace and joy. I learned that these areas that are filled with gold actually are able to reflect our Heavenly Father and in fact, I look just like Him in these areas. Every crack or wound that was not healed are now able to be healed but with the substance that brings wholeness.

Stephanie Rene` Claiborne
WITH FULLNESS OF JOY

I remember when I learned about a Japanese technique where they repair cracked or broken pottery by filling the cracks with pure gold. The method is called *Kintsukuroi*[1], which means: "golden repair". I couldn't believe that I had an encounter that matched a process that was century years old. It will have to become a common process that we undergo freely as we deal with the wounds that we have labored with in our lifetime.

While I was in first year of ministry school, I became open to the Father moving within my heart to bring me to a place where I would deal with each and every issue that would come up. This process can become dirty and messy but the key is to make sure that we don't allow the dirt to go onto others. IF we do have dirt that goes on others, we have to make sure that we clean up our mess in the process. To clean up our mess can be difficult to do and also will cause us to walk in humility within our process. If you think about how a person who is digging for gold can become dirty and will move dirt around and from place to place in order to gain access to the gold. This is the major prize that we want to attain.

I would say that as we look at ourselves and what He wants to do in our hearts, I think that we have to ensure that we are mindful of our soul. We have to make sure that we are surrounded by people who love us and that are able to tell us if we are really messy, or if we are being neglectful of ourselves. There is a real tendency to not take care of ourselves. We can sometimes think that we don't deserve the goodness of God to the point that we end up taking care of others rather than ourselves. This is where I believe that taking communion is essential to the regeneration and longevity of the life of Christ in our lives.

1 My Modern Met Team, "Kintsugi." Last modified April 25, 2017

https://mymodernmet.com/kintsugi-kintsukuroi/ . Accessed October 6,2017.

LOVE, LIFE, AND *Beyond*

Recently, I began taking communion in what I like to call "behind the veil". This literally led me into an encounter where I took the elements in such a reverent and holy manner that I began to see how the Father intended us to remember His Son, Jesus, as the one that would give us life eternal. I used to think that if you didn't have a personal relationship with Christ and took communion just because you wanted to, you would bring a curse upon yourself. I remember thinking that way because of what I was taught as a new believer back in the 1990's. i.e., the scripture that reads *"He who eats and drinks unworthily brings condemnation upon himself, not discerning the Lord's body."* I Corinthians 11:29.

COME INTO UNION WITH HIM

Being in union with the Creator of the Universe holds a special place for us. As we come into union with God, through His son, Jesus, we open ourselves up to a whole new realm of possibilities. Embracing these possibilities is serious business. To decide to enter into this sacred place with Jesus is actually very costly. I have had to let some things go in order to go deeper. Some things have kept me from entering in, such as getting caught up in politics, gossip, or other worldly attitudes and desires. I have noticed that these things keep me tethered to the earth and to the soul instead of being connected with Him.

" Whatever overshadows us we are bound to release." -
Bill Johnson[2]

---

2 Bill Johnson. "The Resting Place", God TV. http://www.god.tv/node/503 . Original air date October 1, 2011. https://youtu.be/lsQmLuG-Exo . Accessed October 6, 2017.

Did you know that if you are allowing anxiety, doubt, unbelief and other ungodly attitudes to overshadow you, you will release them into the environment around you? I have noticed that as I live my life with my mind on Christ and His goodness, I release heaven around me and others are affected. I notice that I am perceptive to the needs around me, to the people around me, and to the atmosphere, which also becomes changed and charged with the frequency of heaven. I remember one time, in a dream, I saw myself in a cavern where there was a pool of water. In this pool were rainbow lights and sounds I have never heard before. The funny thing was that I could see the sounds and the music that was coming up from the pool. Jesus was standing next to me and He said "go ahead and jump in". I did and I was astounded that the light and the sounds were changing my very being. My DNA was changing to reflect more of His DNA and more of His structure. I was made very aware of His kindness and His intention of making me whole. It seems that God desires to have us aligned to not only His ways but to His nature as well. Ever since the fall of mankind, we have struggled to obtain oneness with God in a manner that would reflect His original design for our lives.

WHAT DOES IT ALL MEAN?

What this means is that we have a way into full relationship with God. He has made the way through His Son, Jesus, and this path will bring us into fullness of joy. This joy is literally from God Himself, and will speak to every insecurity, every unrighteous thought, every heartache and every wound. God is secure in who He is, and this will be imparted unto us as we move freely within His love.

We cannot afford to not engage in knowing who He is. It seems to me that He is wanting us to live a life of freedom and of love which will bring us into a place of Rest and Shalom. This is where we must find ourselves willing to take the chance of taking His hands, forsaking the things that keep us tethered to the earth (what we think and know). When we allow ourselves to open our hearts fully to His presence, we are then able to embrace who He is and what He desires for our lives. So just let go of anything that would stand in your way of knowing who He is. Embrace your freedom from pain and past hurts and allow your heavenly Father to fill every single wound with GOLD.

BIBLIOGRAPHY

"Abide." *Dictionary.com*. Unabridged, based on the Random House Dictionary, © *Random House, Inc.*2018. Accessed September 2,2016. www.dictionary.com/browse/abide

Johnson, Bill. "The Resting Place", God TV. http://www.god.tv/node/503 . Original air date October 1, 2011. Accessed October 6, 2017. https://youtu.be/lsQmLuG-Exo

My Modern Met Team, "Kintsugi." Last modified April 25, 2017. https://mymodernmet.com/kintsugi-kintsukuroi/. Accessed October 6,2017.

"North." Dictionary.com. The American Heritage ® Idioms Dictionary. Copyright © 2002, 2001, 1995 by Houghton Mifflin Company. Published by Houghton Mifflin Company. Accessed August 30. 2017. www.dictionary.com/browse/find-true-north

RESOURCES

The author suggests the following resources.

Stephanie Claiborne-
Author Fullness Of Joy
Speaker and Life Coach at Heart Of Gold
Website: www.heartofgoldministries.com

Stephanie believes that because the Father is good and the nature of God is to be good all of the time, we then are allowed to be in a space where we can live in the knowledge of who He is. With this knowledge, we then can impart the Father's heart to others as Stephanie has learned this in her own personal journey. This has made Stephanie, and others who live by this principle spiritual goldminers with a kingdom reality.

Stephanie enjoys finding the gold and believing the very best in others. This is because we have been made in the image of God- who is good. This is why Stephanie believes that it is important to champion people so that their true selves are displayed.

Throughout Stephanie's life, she has been able to persevere through adversity and challenges. In her earlier years, Stephanie was not so graceful in doing so, but now, she able to understand that the circumstances that are around her are meant to bring out the best in not only herself, but in others. This core belief is what will make us unstoppable to various trials.

Relationships and community are vital as this has been shown to us in the bible. Stephanie is dedicated and passionate about building and bringing family and community in all spheres of influence, i.e. family, education, faith, business, and government. Stephanie also believes that there is no community without unity. Stephanie truly believes that we will thrive when we bring a since of unity into a full kingdom reality. This will come from a place of abiding and oneness with our Creator.

Stephanie is not only passionate about seeing revival in our communities, she is passionate to see reformation take place as well. This is where she says we will see Heaven displayed here on earth.

Stephanie is also engaged in prayer and intersession for homes, neighborhoods, communities and nations This is how the kingdom of God is revealed in the earth and how divine alignment can take place. We then become the watchmen and the repairer of the breach.

Stephanie has been able to marry intercession with business and has been able to move in a manner that brings glory to God. This is displayed by seeing how the practical business practices along with spiritual understanding can marry each other in order to bring a higher level of operating that brings glory to God.

The most important aspect of all of this is having the heart of the heart of the Good Samaritan. Stephanie believes that in helping our neighbors to live in a manner that brings fullness of His presence and reveals our true selves, is of the most importance.

All of this has shaped Stephanie into the person that she has become. Stephanie is connected with a vital prison ministry in the state of Alaska and is passionate about people understanding who they are and letting the Father reveal and unveil who they really are.

Stephanie would love to champion you, whether that is in the form of speaking engagements, workshops, or coaching. Vendors looking to distribute Stephanie Claiborne's book Fullness of Joy, email us at stephanie@heartofgoldministries.com

Liz Wright-

Author Ekklesia Rising
Founder & Senior Director of
The Bridal Company
Website: http://thebridalcompany.org/

Liz has been gifted as an oracle to speak from Jesus heart truths to set us free, to activate encounters and to release Heaven's perspective. She lives to know Gods love and to help people from every walk of life become confident, powerful and whole as they experience His love for themselves and come to see the immense value of who they really are.

Liz is the founder and senior director of *The Bridal Company* and in this capacity, serves as a spiritual adviser, an author and speaks both nationally and internationally. Liz is the author of "*Ekklesia Rising*", the sought after, groundbreaking publication that unlocks the mystery of our life's calling to abide in Christ. She is currently writing Volume 2 in the series and is working on the development of media projects, all with the objective of helping people experience the Presence of Jesus and become all they were created to be.

In her advisory capacity, Liz works with leaders and organizations, helping to direct the development of strategic prayer to see established their respective visions and mandates. Liz's mandate in this office is to see

the Kingdom of God become the principal
influence over each work and sphere of society.

EKKLESIA RISING by Liz Wright
Visitations From Jesus
Revealing The Truth And Power Of Who We
Really Are"

We are rising out of the ashes of pain and
powerless religion, becoming a pure reflection
of God in the earth. Destined to be fully filled
with His beautiful, powerful Spirit we are
together, an emerging unstoppable force of love
and transforming authority.

A people the realm of darkness cannot prevail
against.

As we learn to abide, experiencing and yielding
to His life changing indwelling Presence, we
receive the ability to live out of who we truly are
in Christ. We find His Spirit increasingly
flowing through us to heal and align every
aspect of our life and identity with truth and to
restore every hurting life we touch.

Where life's challenges, the brokenness in
others or the enemies lies have defined you and
held you captive, as you read the heart and
wisdom of Jesus contained within these pages
the eyes of your understanding will be flooded
with light. You will become empowered to
experience a level of freedom and peace you
never thought possible. With a renewed security
in the absolute love of God, you will be set free
to live out of your authentic self and so begin to
produce your highest purpose.

We are Children of Light, Carriers of God, we are the most valuable, powerful thing in all of creation.

You can purchase Liz's book *Ekklesia Rising* **here**: https://www.amazon.com/Ekklesia-Rising-Visitations-revealing-really-ebook/dp/B00XPOC0J2

Destiny House and Jennifer A. Miskov, Ph. D: Destiny House is a Levite tribe of worshipers leading people into life changing encounters with Jesus. Our one desire is to know God more. We believe that destinies are birthed from a place of intimacy with God and connection to family. Our dream is to raise up an army of Jesus lovers who live in total surrender and who love God wholeheartedly.

We have a 100-year vision for worship to be released in the context of family at Destiny House Redding and for 5,000 other worshiping communities to be launched around the world. Influenced by *Silver to Gold* (by Jennifer A. Miskov) and modeled after Carrie Judd Montgomery's healing home, *Home of Peace*, we believe Destiny House will be a significant place where God's presence is cultivated and where missionaries, leaders, and women revivalists will be healed, restored, empowered to thrive in the John 10:10 promise, and launched into a greater measure of their destinies.

As part of our 100- year vision we hold weekly worship meetings every Friday. Come and join our family! Our address is *2391 Placer Street, Redding, CA.*

Jennifer A. Miskov Ph.D.: Jennifer A. Miskov, Ph.D., is the founding director of Destiny House, a ministry that cultivates communities of worshippers who do life together in God's presence and who launch people into their destinies from a place of intimacy with God and connection with family.

Jen, a bodyboarder from Southern California, graduated from Vanguard University in 2000 and then immediately following this, went to Mozambique, Africa to work with the poor for six months with Iris Ministries. She later returned to Orange County and spent 5 years working with Starbucks, eventually as a trainer and manager before quitting her job, selling her car, and moving to England to follow one of her dreams. She recently graduated from the University of Birmingham, UK with a PhD and relocated back to California. She is passionate about helping people live their true and full destinies and mentoring people in their passions.

Jen has supported Bill Johnson in his *Defining Moments* book as well as authored *Walking on Water, Ignite Azusa: Positioning for a New Jesus Revolution, Writing in the Glory, Life on Wings, Spirit Flood, and Silver to Gold.* Jen teaches a revival history class at Bethel School of Supernatural Ministry as well as facilitates Writing in the Glory workshops at Destiny House and around the world. Jen is ordained by Heidi Baker with Iris Global and is also licensed with Bethel Church of Redding, California. Jen loves to lead people into a greater lifestyle of union with Jesus through her writing, teaching, and ministry. She received her Ph.D. in Global Pentecostal and Charismatic Studies from the University of Birmingham, U.K.

Learn more of Jennifer Miskov's transformational books here...
http://www.silvertogold.com/store/

Marie Fowler:
Founder of All Glorious Within and author of
Living Stones
Website:
https://allgloriouswithincom.wordpress.com/

Marie Fowler's greatest passion is to spend her life at the feet of her extravagant King. Awakened to love at an early age through what would become a lifetime of transformational encounters, Marie lives and ministers from a place of deep intimacy and identity. Whether it be through small home fellowships, worship communities, or houses of prayer, Marie releases revelation and edification to the Bride about her true identity, calling her to awaken to the glory of God within.

Marie is a passionate lover of Israel, advocate, and intercessor. God began to awaken Marie in her own spiritual journey by revealing His heart for Israel and the Jewish people. Marie is dedicated to the restoration of the whole house of Israel: Jew and Gentile, One in Messiah Yeshua (Jesus). She passionately teaches about the One New Man Movement (Ezekiel 37: 1-23 and Ephesians 2:15) and is fully invested in seeing this End-Time Movement come to a glorious full-term birth! Her heart is to release the One New Man (Jew and Gentile) into their truest identity and thus see God's Holy Habitation built- *Living Stone* upon *Living Stone.*

Living Stones by Marie Fowler: Discover your true identity in this groundbreaking depth study on the **12 Tribes of Israel**.

Throughout the ages Creation has been groaning for identity, dominion, and ultimately restored intimacy and communion with the Father. If we are in Christ, we are a new creation. We are made in His image. But what does it mean to be made in His image? Who am I as a new creation? What is my destiny? Desperately seeking on her own journey of identity, author Marie Fowler spent twenty-five years researching the tribes of Israel to answer these questions.
Our heavenly Father designed us for one sole purpose: habitation. God chooses to build His house through His family. Living Stones is a love letter in which you will discover your place within God's family. Worship (intimacy) reveals identity. One does not come face-to-face with someone and remain unaltered. As we encounter the Father with unveiled faces, we become like Him. Our utmost destiny is that we might take on His reflection found in the embodiment of habitation.

Join Marie in her fascinating and biblically grounded study of the tribes of Israel as foundational keys to reveal every believer's identity in Christ. Watch in wonder as the author explains with amazing prophetic and revelatory insight how the characteristics of each tribe fit together as living stones displaying the facets of the Father's nature and character thereby building His holy habitation.

Get your copy of Living Stones here…
https://allgloriouswithin.ecwid.com/Living-Stones-Your-Journey-Into-Habitation-with-the-Living-God-p82294474

Made in the USA
Middletown, DE
06 November 2018